Let's Pray Together

Creating a Legacy of Prayer

By Carol Graves

Additional copies of this book can be ordered online at
www.fullyinfocus.com
e-mail - fullyinfocus@yahoo.com

Contents

About the Author

Carol Graves has a God given passion to encourage and equip people of all ages to discover the fullness of God and the power of focused prayer. Her devotional books, *Fully in Focus - A Scriptural Collection Illustrating the Attributes of God,* and *Fully in Focus – Discovering the Fullness of God*, offer over 100 glimpses of God's character found in God's Word, the Bible. Equipping readers with a knowledge of God's character and a focus on praise, these books help shift the focus of prayer from what you can do to what God can do.

Her Bible study, *Four Steps to Peace – The Journey,* explores four steps of prayer: Praise, Repent, Acknowledge and Yield, resulting in the "peace that passes all understanding." The study is focused on God's Word and has both refreshed and transformed the prayer life of many.

The desire to build a foundation of faith in children led Carol to write five children's books, all designed to teach children about God's character and encourage them to grow in their knowledge and faith in God. Carol has been awarded two Christian Choice Book Awards.

The importance of creating a legacy of prayer inspired Carol to write *Let's Pray Together.* Praying for our children and praying with our children promises to create an example of faith as well as establish a relationship based on the truth of God. The power of prayer is a legacy that will influence generations of the future as well as establish a peace and hope in the present.

Carol is an Area Coordinator for Moms in Prayer International, a frequent speaker for Stonecroft Ministries, MOPs Ministries, and various other ministries. She leads Life Groups in her local church and has been featured on U2HaveHope radio ministry. Carol is the mother of three children and the grandmother of three. She and her husband Dave live in San Antonio, Texas.

A note from Carol

When did you learn to pray? Perhaps you remember childhood prayers such as "God is great. God is good. Let us thank Him for our food." Perhaps you prayed "Now I lay me down to sleep…" before bedtime. Although these simple recited prayers are a way to introduce prayer to small children, how do we help them grow in their prayer life? Perhaps you are one of the many adults I have encountered who tell me, "I just don't know how to pray."

This book is designed to help you develop a "prayer relationship" with a child and to teach them about prayer. Just as we guide our children in their behaviors, in their choices, in their relationships, showing them how to grow in their relationship with God through prayer will be a lasting legacy that will establish the foundation of a maturing faith. Never will you become closer to a child as when you spend time with them sharing your hearts in prayer. As you learn to focus on God, you will experience a growing faith and your conversations in prayer will result in the peace described in *Philippians 4:7a (NLT) "Then you will experience God's peace, which exceeds anything we can understand."*

Read the introduction, then with the child read the age appropriate introduction for children. As you pray together, record your prayer thoughts, then occasionally look back at your journal entries together and record how you are seeing God work in response to your prayers. This will help the child understand that God is real, He is living and He cares about each of us in a very personal way.

Take advantage of opportunities to pray together through the years. At those times when the child needs encouragement or faces fears, or at times of blessing or victory, take time to pray with them. **Investing your time and love in their life will pay priceless dividends as you create a legacy of prayer.**

Introduction

What is prayer?

In the dictionary "prayer" is defined as "a humble and sincere request to God; an utterance to God in praise, thanksgiving, confession; any spiritual communion with God." To put it simply, prayer is talking with God. A prayer can be a long conversation with God or as short as one word. ***Help your child understand that prayer not just talking to God, it is a conversation with God.***

All too often our prayers become only a list of requests. How would you feel if your child never said, "I love you" or "I'm sorry" or "thank you?" How would your child feel if you never spoke those words - if the only communication either of you heard was a list of "I want" or "I need." Teaching your child to pray using four simple steps will nourish your personal relationship as well as grow in your relationship with God.

The four steps can be remembered by the word "**PRAY.**"

Praise. Repent. Acknowledge. Yield.

Praise - *O Lord, I will honor and praise your name, for you are my God. You do such wonderful things! You planned them long ago, and now you have accomplished them. Isaiah 25:1 (NLT)*

Begin prayer by praising God for who He is. Praise is not thanking God for what He has done, it springs from knowing who He is. Each journal page starts with an attribute of God that is defined and illustrated with a scripture. As you or your child reads the definition, talk about what that attribute means in relationship to who God is. Read the scripture together and see that God's Word tells about God's character.

Discuss how this applies to your life. When you are ready, spend some time together praising God. Just simple phrases such as "God I praise You for you are good and You want what is best for us." "God I praise you that you are dependable and I know You are always with me." Give your child opportunity to praise God in his/her own words. As you model what praise sounds like, you will find that your child will follow your example. When you finish, in the journal lines, write a simple statement of praise to God.

Repent – It is vital that you teach your child how important this step is. God's Word clearly states that we are all sinners. *Romans 3:23 (NLT) "For everyone has sinned; we all fall short of God's glorious standard."* It is important that we understand that we all have sin in common – both parents and children. I appreciate Paul's confession found in **Romans 7:18-19 (NLT)** *"And I know that nothing good lives in me, that is, in my sinful nature. I want to do what is right, but I can't. I want to do what is good, but I don't. I don't want to do what is wrong, but I do it anyway."*

If your child understands and acknowledges their sin, yet has not prayed to receive Jesus Christ as Lord and Savior, this would be a wonderful opportunity to share your testimony and possibly lead your child to receive the gift of salvation. A simple plan of salvation referred to as the Romans Road can be found in the last pages of this journal.

The importance of acknowledging our sin, confessing it to God and repenting (turning away from sin) in respect to our prayer life is stated in *Isaiah 59:2 (NLT) "It's your sins that have cut you off from God. Because of your sins, he has turned away and will not listen anymore."* The good news is found in *1 John 1:9 (NLT) "But if we confess our sins to him, he is faithful and just to forgive us our sins and to cleanse us from all wickedness."*

Confession and repentance is very personal. It is required by all, both young and old. A time of silent confession can be introduced by simply reading the scripture verse, explaining it in simple terms or discussing it, then spending a few moments in silence.

9

Guidance for repentance is clearly stated in *1 John 5:21 (NLT) "Dear children, keep away from anything that might take God's place in your hearts."*

Acknowledge - It is always nice to hear the words, "Thank you," but how much more does it mean when it is followed by, "I know that you put much time and thought into this and I appreciate it so very much." We are honored when our efforts are acknowledged. So often we prompt our children to say "thank you" but we do not teach them to be grateful and appreciative of the time and treasure they receive.

We see that God considers thankfulness a sacrifice that we can offer to Him in *Psalm 50:14a and 23a (NLT) "Make thankfulness your sacrifice to God." "But giving thanks is a sacrifice that truly honors me."*

To sacrifice means to give something up. What are we giving up when offer a sacrifice of thankfulness to God? We are giving up our pride. We are acknowledging that God is the source of all provision and blessing. When we humble ourselves and declare as the Psalmist did in **Psalms 100:3-5**, we honor God as He alone deserves. *"Acknowledge that the LORD is God! He made us, and we are his. We are his people, the sheep of his pasture. Enter his gates with thanksgiving; go into his courts with praise. Give thanks to him and praise his name. For the LORD is good. His unfailing love continues forever, and his faithfulness continues to each generation."*

Even when things don't turn out like we have hoped, or when we don't receive those things we desire, we are to acknowledge God and give Him thanks, knowing that His plan is perfect and that He wants only good for us. *"Be thankful in all circumstances, for this is God's will for you who belong to Christ Jesus."* 1 Thessalonians 5:18 (NLT)

Having an attitude of gratitude even for the simple everyday things honors God. Teaching your child to include this in their prayers will also teach them to see the goodness of God in all things. Model this

10

attitude of thanksgiving and acknowledging God as you pray with your child. Once again, it will help them see that God is a part of every moment of every day. Journal the blessings and the ways that you are grateful.

Yield – Many times when we pray, we only "ask." If you look back at the first three steps of prayer, it becomes clear that our focus has not been on our needs, but on the One who is able to meet those needs. As we praise God for who He is, we see that there is nothing too difficult for Him. As we confess our sin and repent, we know that He forgives our sin and when we come to Him with a clean heart He hears our prayer. As we acknowledge and give thanks to God, we are reminded of all the ways God has worked in our lives. This fills us with a confident trust as we bring our requests to Him.

This last step of prayer is the time to express our needs, seek guidance, and voice our requests to God. But more than just "asking" we must "yield" our concerns to God. As we voice our requests, we must trust God to do His work in His perfect way and in His perfect time. Our desire should be that God will answer our prayers according to His perfect will and in a way that will bring Him glory. Smaller children may not understand this, but as you pray with them, you are modeling your faith and trust in God.

Keep this book and use it often. Encourage your child to pray specifically. Many times we forget what we have prayed for so, record these specific requests, then as you occasionally look back at the journal entries, record how God has specifically answered the prayers you have prayed together. This will encourage a growing relationship with God, showing that He is real and personal. In later years, at an appropriate time, give this book to the child who became your prayer partner. It will be a testament to God's faithfulness and love and hopefully will inspire a desire to continue creating a legacy of prayer in the life of another child.

Introduction for Small Children

This book is called a journal. It is a special book we can use to learn about God and write about the times we talk to Him together. When we talk to God it is called prayer. Just like you and I talk to each other, we can talk to God. We are going to learn some ways that we can talk to God that will help us know more about Him. God wants us to talk to Him because He loves us.

When we talk to God together, the first thing we will do is learn about who God is. The Bible helps us learn about God so we will read a Bible verse about Him, then we will begin to talk to Him in a special way called **"PRAISE."** When I tell you that you are kind to your friends, I am praising you for who you are. When you tell me that I am strong or smart or that I am special, you are praising me. God likes for us to know all about Him and the more we learn, the more we can praise Him.

After we praise God, we will ask God to help us remember anything that we have done that would make Him sad. At times we all do wrong things and that is called sin. God wants us to confess. That means tell Him when we do wrong things so that He can forgive us. God asks us to **"REPENT."** That means turn our back and walk away from doing wrong and choose to do right. God hears our prayers when we confess and repent of our sin.

Next we will talk about all the special ways that God has worked in our lives and blessed us. We will say "thank you" to Him and **"ACKNOWLEDGE"** the many ways He blesses us.

The last part of our prayer will be our time to ask God to help us with our needs. Ask God specifically for what it is you need. God always knows what is best, so after we ask, we must **"YIELD"** and let Him decide how to answer our prayer.

We will write the things we talk with God about in this book and when you are older, as you read what we have written it will help you remember how we learned about God and prayed together.

Each time we pray together, we will
PRAISE, REPENT, ACKNOWLEDGE, AND YIELD.

Let's write down the first letter of each of those words and see what it spells.

_____ _____ _____ _____

If you are ready, let's talk to God.

Introduction for Older Children

Prayer is simply a conversation with God. Just as you might converse with a few of your friends, you, your prayer partner and God can have a conversation. Often we think of prayer as a time to ask God for things. Prayer can become much more meaningful and powerful when we learn to approach God with our focus on Him rather than on our problems or our needs. Learning about God's character through reading scriptures from the Bible helps us see that God's love for us is the foundation of all that He is. From that unfailing love springs the attributes that you will read about in this journal.

The purpose of this journal is twofold. First it will equip you and your prayer partner to grow in your relationship and understanding of each other as you spend time together in prayer. Second, it will serve as a record of your spiritual growth as you learn to pray with purpose and see God's response to your prayers. Your parent or grandparent would be an ideal prayer partner. As you join in prayer, your relationship will become something you will treasure in future years.

As you pray together, first read the scripture and definition of the attribute of God and focus on who He is. Share how God has revealed Himself in your lives. As you focus on God's character, offer **PRAISE** to God. Praise is not thanking God for what He has done, it springs from knowing who He is. Learning to praise God and know who He is enables your confidence and trust in Him to grow. Write a simple statement of praise to God in the journal to remind you of who He is.

Just as you might not want to face your parent when you know you have done something wrong, it is difficult to come before God with known behaviors that are not pleasing to God. A willingness to confess and **REPENT** of any known sin enables your relationship with God to grow and when you pray with a clean heart, God hears your prayer. This time of confession should be silent and personal. Together, read the scripture,

14

then silently ask God to reveal any behavior that offends Him and choose to turn away from that behavior with God's help.

We all like to hear a "thank you" when we help someone or give them a gift. But hearing them acknowledge your hard work or sacrifice is much more meaningful. Yes, we experience blessings each day, but do we **ACKNOWLEDGE** that God is the source of those blessings? Learning to thank God and acknowledge daily blessings will help you see Him and His work in your life in new and exciting ways. In the journal, record the ways that God has blessed you.

As you can see, so far this conversation with God has been focused on Him. We have praised Him, repented and received His forgiveness, acknowledged His work and blessings and now we are ready to bring our needs to Almighty God who is able to meet our every need. Our focus can shift from our needs and what we can do to our God and what He can do! When you pray, ask God specifically for what you need. With confidence, trust and faith, we can bring our cares and concerns before God, then **YIELD** those cares and concerns to Him. It is a picture of letting Him go before us. To yield means to "give up." That is what God wants us to do. He wants us to give up our cares and concerns and let Him work according to His will and in ways that will bring Him glory. God answers all of our prayers. The answer is not always what we expect, but it is always for our good. We must trust His perfect will and His perfect timing.

So remember as you talk with God,
P R A Y.
Praise, Repent, Acknowledge, Yield.

Record your conversations and God's responses in this journal and one day you may look back and see how God has heard your every prayer and answered in ways that are a reflection of His love.

15

What Others Have Said About Prayer

Nothing tends more to cement the hearts of Christians than praying together. Never do they love one another so well as when they witness the outpouring of each other's hearts in prayer.
Charles Finney

*When we bring God's Word into our prayer,
we bring His power into our prayer.*
Joni Erickson Tada

*Any concern too small to be turned into a prayer
is too small to be made into a burden.*
Corrie Ten Boom

The prayer of the feeblest saint on earth who lives in the spirit and keeps right with God is a terror to Satan. The very powers of darkness are paralyzed by prayer... No wonder Satan tries to keep our minds fussy in active work till we cannot think in prayer.
Oswald Chambers

*Our prayers lay the track down on which God's power can come.
Like a mighty locomotive His power is irresistible,
But is cannot reach us without rails.*
Watchman Nee

Prayer is where the action is.
John Wesley

Prayer is the inheritance we receive and the legacy we leave.
Mark Batterson

Let's Pray Together
Creating a Legacy of Prayer

This book was inspired by my desire to create a legacy of prayer for my family. I purchased a journal for each of my grandchildren and asked if they would spend a few moments with me in prayer. What a blessing to see their willingness and hear their simple, sincere conversations with God. Now, each time we are together, we spend some time learning about who God is and joining together in prayer. In future years, perhaps at a significant moment in their life, I hope to give this book back to them, filled with praises, prayers and God's answers.

I wrote this book to equip and encourage you as you create a legacy of prayer. Surely there were people in the past of whom you have no knowledge who prayed for you as one of the future generation. You can be a part of a continuing legacy for generations to come as you pray together with a child.

Each section in the book features a definition and three scriptures that focus on an attribute of God's character. The definition will enable a clearer understanding of exactly what the attribute means. The first scripture focuses on praise, the second on repentance and the last is a springboard of encouragement. Learning about God's character builds a foundation of faith and trust in God that brings about a confident peace. As you read the scriptures, I encourage you to discuss your thoughts, then pray together and journal your thoughts and prayers. My prayer is that God will bless you and future generations as you create a legacy of prayer.

Date: _____

God is Able

Able: having sufficient power, intelligence, competence, skill to accomplish action

If we are thrown into the blazing furnace, the God whom we serve is able to save us. He will rescue us from your power, Your Majesty.
Daniel 3:17 (NLT)

In the Bible, we read about three men, Shadrach, Meshach and Abed-nego who refused to worship idols. They were told they would be thrown into a furnace of blazing fire if they did not obey the King. They declared that they would not worship idols. They trusted that God was able to keep them from burning, and He did! There are many more accounts in the Bible that show us how God is able to do things we cannot do. Knowing that God is able to protect and provide for us gives reason to praise Him.

Praise

_____

_____

_____

_____

_____

Repent

Therefore, put on every piece of God's armor so you will be able to resist the enemy in the time of evil. Then after the battle you will still be standing firm. Ephesians 6:13 (NLT)

God is Able

Acknowledge

_____
_____
_____
_____
_____
_____

Yield

_____
_____
_____
_____
_____
_____

Now all glory to God, who is able, through his mighty power at work within us to accomplish infinitely more than we might ask or think.
Ephesians 3:20 (NLT)

How did God respond to this prayer?

_____
_____
_____
_____
_____
_____
_____

God Answers

Answer: a response to a question, problem or need

You faithfully answer our prayers with awesome deeds, O God our savior. You are the hope of everyone on earth, even those who sail on distant seas. Psalm 65:5 (NLT)

My grandson was in the car with me and I had mentioned that after picking up his sister we might go to his favorite play place for lunch. Over and over again he asked, "Are we going there?" I answered, "We'll see." Again he continued to ask, "Grandma, can we have lunch there?" I answered, "We might." After several times back and forth, he finally said, "Grandma, just say YES!" It seemed that he did not think I had answered until I said "YES." So often when we pray, we ask, and we expect a "YES." God wants what is best for us. Praise God that He answers all of our prayers – sometimes with a "yes," sometimes He says, "not now," and His answer is always perfect – even when the answer is "no."

Praise

_____
_____
_____
_____
_____

Repent

Brothers, listen! We are here to proclaim that through this man Jesus there is forgiveness for your sins. Acts 13:38 (NLT)

God Answers

Acknowledge

_____
_____
_____
_____
_____
_____

Yield

_____
_____
_____
_____
_____

This is what the LORD says, he who made the earth, the LORD who formed it and established it—the LORD is his name: "Call to me, and I will answer you, and tell you great and unsearchable things you do not know." Jeremiah 33:2-3 (NIV)

How did God respond to this prayer?

_____
_____
_____
_____
_____
_____

Date: _____

God is the source of Blessing

Blessing: enjoying great happiness; special benefit or favor

All praise to God, the Father of our Lord Jesus Christ, who has blessed us with every spiritual blessing in the heavenly realms because we are united with Christ. Ephesians 1:3 (NLT)

God enjoys blessing his children. The blessings He gives us make us happy. Not all blessings are "material things." The very best blessings are "spiritual blessings" such as love, joy, and peace. Although these are not things we can touch or see, we are happiest when God gives us these "spiritual blessings." These special blessings come from God and we can have His love, joy and peace all the time. If we obey God, His blessings are guaranteed. Praise God for the many ways He blesses.

Praise

_____
_____
_____
_____
_____
_____
_____

Repent
Walk with the wise and become wise; associate with fools and get in trouble. Trouble chases sinners, while blessings reward the righteous. Proverbs 13:20-22 (NLT)

God is the source of Blessing

Acknowledge

_____
_____
_____
_____
_____
_____

Yield

_____
_____
_____
_____
_____

May the Lord continually bless you, with heaven's blessings
as well as with human joys.
Psalm 128:5 (TLB)

How did God respond to this prayer?

_____
_____
_____
_____
_____
_____

God Builds

Build: to make by putting together; to order, plan or direct the construction of; to cause to be or grow; create; develop

For every house has a builder, but the one who built everything is God.
Hebrews 3:4(NLT)

Everything has been built by God. He built the entire universe, the stars, the planets, the sun, and the moon. He created all things, the plants, the animals, the birds, the fish, the oceans, and the mountains. He formed our bodies that function perfectly. Take time to praise God for all of His amazing creation. Praise God that He builds us up and does not tear us down.

Praise

_____
_____
_____
_____
_____
_____
_____
_____

Repent

But anyone who hears my teaching and doesn't obey it is foolish, like a
person who builds a house on sand.
Matthew 7:26 (NLT)

God Builds

Acknowledge

_____

_____

_____

_____

_____

_____

Yield

_____

_____

_____

_____

_____

_____

And now I entrust you, to God and the message of his grace
that is able to build you up and give you an inheritance
with all those he has set apart for himself.
Acts 20:32 (NLT)

How did God respond to this prayer?

_____

_____

_____

_____

_____

_____

God is Caring

Caring: to feel concern or interest; to look after or provide for

Come, let us bow down in worship, let us kneel before the LORD our Maker; for He is our God and we are the people of his pasture, the flock under his care. Psalm 95:6-7a (NLT)

God uses the example of a shepherd caring for his sheep very often in the Bible. A shepherd is a person who takes care of his sheep. He makes sure that they have food and water. He protects them from harm. If they are fearful he calms them and if they get hurt, he tends to their wounds. Jesus is called the "Good Shepherd." He loves us, provides for us, protects us and cares for us in every way. He is interested in every moment of every day. He is looking after you because He cares for you. Praise God that He is caring.

Praise

_____
_____
_____
_____
_____

Repent
I will be glad and rejoice in your unfailing love, for you have seen my troubles, and you care about the anguish of my soul.
Psalm 31:7 (NLT)

God is Caring

Acknowledge

_____
_____
_____
_____
_____
_____
_____

Yield

_____
_____
_____
_____
_____
_____

Give all your worries and cares to God, for he cares about you.
1 Peter 5:7 (NLT)

How did God respond to this prayer?

_____
_____
_____
_____
_____
_____
_____

Date: _____

God is Compassionate

Compassion: showing loving sympathy; sorrow for the trouble of others accompanied by an urge to help

Sing for joy, O heavens! Rejoice, O earth! Burst into song, O mountains! For the LORD has comforted his people and will have compassion on them in their suffering. Isaiah 49:13 (NLT)

When a friend is hurt or having a hard time, it is natural to feel sorry for them. If you are a good friend, you will want to help them. The Bible tells us that Jesus showed compassion on many people who were suffering. He saw that some people were in trouble and needed help. He felt sorry for people who were sick. He cried when he learned that his friend had died. But he did not just feel sorry for them, He helped them with their needs in many different ways. Praise God that He is loving and compassionate. He wants to help when you have troubles.

Praise

_____
_____
_____
_____
_____

Repent

Once again you will have compassion on us. You will trample our sins under your feet and throw them into the depths of the ocean! Micah 7:19 (NLT)

God is Compassionate

Acknowledge

_____
_____
_____
_____
_____
_____

Yield

_____
_____
_____
_____
_____

The LORD is good to everyone.
He showers compassion on all his creation.
Psalm 145:9 (NLT)

How did God respond to this prayer?

_____
_____
_____
_____
_____
_____

God Corrects

Correct: to change from wrong to right; to point our errors or faults

All Scripture is inspired by God and is useful to teach us what is true and to make us realize what is wrong in our lives. It corrects us when we are wrong and teaches us to do what is right. 2 Timothy 3:16 (NLT)

What would happen if a person thought a red stoplight meant "go" and a green stoplight meant "stop?" There would probably be many accidents. That person would need to be corrected so everyone would be safe. Wouldn't it be sad if you thought that God does not love you? The Bible tells us over and over again that God loves us. God gave us the Bible to teach us how to act and correct us when we think and do wrong things. When we follow God's Word and correct those things we do wrong, we receive His blessing. Praise God that He corrects us because He loves us.

Praise

_____

_____

_____

_____

_____

Repent

Search me, O God, and know my heart; test me and know my anxious thoughts. Point out anything in me that offends you, and lead me along the path of everlasting life.
Psalms 39:23-24 (NLT)

God Corrects

Acknowledge

_____
_____
_____
_____
_____
_____

Yield

_____
_____
_____
_____
_____

For the LORD corrects those he loves,
just as a father corrects a child in whom he delights.
Proverbs 3:12 (NLT)

How did God respond to this prayer?

_____
_____
_____
_____
_____
_____
_____
_____

God is our Defender

Defender: one who guards from attack; to protect from harm or danger

For the angel of the LORD is a guard;
he surrounds and defends all who fear him.
Psalm 34:7 (NLT)

An enemy is someone who wants to harm us in some way. The enemy of God is Satan. Jesus faced Satan who tempted Him to sin, but Jesus answered Satan by speaking God's Word. The truth of God's Word defended Jesus from Satan's attack. We can trust God to protect us and defend us when we face temptations or danger. Praise God that He is a mighty defender. He wins the victory against the enemy.

Praise

_____
_____
_____
_____
_____
_____
_____
_____

Repent

Come with great power, O God, and rescue me!
Defend me with your might.
Psalm 54:1 (NLT)

God is our Defender

Acknowledge

_____
_____
_____
_____
_____
_____

Yield

_____
_____
_____
_____
_____

End the evil of those who are wicked, and defend the righteous. For you look deep within the mind and heart, O righteous God.
Psalm 7:9 (NLT)

How did God respond to this prayer?

_____
_____
_____
_____
_____
_____
_____

God is our Deliverer

Deliver: to set free or save from evil or danger; to rescue

I love you, Lord, my strength. The Lord is my rock, my fortress and my deliverer; my God is my rock, in whom I take refuge, my shield and the horn of my salvation, my stronghold. I called to the Lord who is worthy of praise, and I have been saved from my enemies.
Psalm 18:1-3 (NIV)

When something is delivered, it is taken out of one place and put into another. That is what God can do when we trust Him in times of trouble. God will deliver us from fear, from danger or from temptation. God takes us out of the place of danger and delivers us to a place of peace. We simply must obey Him so that we can be delivered. Praise God that He is our deliverer.

Praise

_____
_____
_____
_____
_____
_____

Repent

Help us, God our Savior, for the glory of your name;
deliver us and forgive our sins for your name's sake.
Psalm 79:9 (NIV)

God is our Deliverer

Acknowledge

_____
_____
_____
_____
_____
_____

Yield

_____
_____
_____
_____
_____

I sought the Lord, and he answered me;
He delivered me from all my fears.
Psalm 34:4 (NIV)

How did God respond to this prayer?

_____
_____
_____
_____
_____
_____
_____

God is Dependable

Dependable: reliable; trustworthy; to be sure of

God is not a man, so he does not lie. He is not human, so he does not change his mind. Has he ever spoken and failed to act? Has he ever promised and not carried it through?
Numbers 23:19 (NLT)

When someone makes a promise to you, you want to be sure that they keep that promise. In the same way, it is important to keep the promises you make to others. If you always do what you say you will do, you are dependable. You can trust that God will keep His promises. He does not lie or say one thing and do another. Praise God that He is dependable. He will never leave you.

Praise

_____
_____
_____
_____
_____
_____

Repent

So now, come back to your God. Act with love and justice, and always depend on him. Hosea 12:6 (NLT)

God is Dependable

Acknowledge

_____
_____
_____
_____
_____
_____

Yield

_____
_____
_____
_____
_____

The LORD is good to those who depend on him,
to those who search for him.
Lamentations 3:25 (NLT)

How did God respond to this prayer?

_____
_____
_____
_____
_____
_____
_____
_____

God Encourages

Encourage: to give courage, hope or confidence; to give support to; be favorable to

I bow before your holy Temple as I worship. I praise your name for your unfailing love and faithfulness; for your promises are backed by all the honor of your name. As soon as I pray, you answer me; you encourage me by giving me strength. Psalm 138:2-3 (NLT)

We all need encouragement. God encourages us because we know that He will always love us, He is always with us, He wants to bless us, and He will forgive us. There are so many other ways God encourages us and we can learn more about God when we read the Bible. Knowing more about God puts courage in us. Praise God that He encourages. We can follow His example and encourage others.

Praise

_____
_____
_____
_____
_____

Repent

Some people brought to him a paralyzed man on a mat. Seeing their faith, Jesus said to the paralyzed man, "Be encouraged, my child! Your sins are forgiven." Matthew 9:2 (NLT)

God Encourages

Acknowledge

_____
_____
_____
_____
_____
_____

Yield

_____
_____
_____
_____
_____

The humble will see their God at work and be glad.
Let all who seek God's help be encouraged.
Psalm 69:32 (NLT)

How did God respond to this prayer?

_____
_____
_____
_____
_____
_____

God Equips

Equips: to prepare for a particular situation or task; to provide, supply or train

All Scripture is inspired by God and is useful to teach us what is true and to make us realize what is wrong in our lives. It corrects us when we are wrong and teaches us to do what is right. God uses it to prepare and equip his people to do every good work.
2 Timothy 3:16-17 (NLT)

God loves us so much that He inspired men who knew Him to write the Bible. God knew we would need instructions so that we could live a happy life. God wanted us to know about Him and how much He loves us. The Bible gives us instructions and encouragement that equips us to live a life that honors God. Praise God that He equips.

Praise

_____

_____

_____

_____

Repent

Prove by the way you live
that you have repented of your sins
and turned to God.
Matthew 3:8 (NLT)

God Equips

Acknowledge

_____
_____
_____
_____
_____
_____

Yield

_____
_____
_____
_____
_____

Now may the God of peace— may he equip you with all you need for doing his will. May he produce in you, through the power of Jesus Christ, every good thing that is pleasing to him. All glory to him forever and ever! Amen. Hebrews 13:20a-21 (NLT)

How did God respond to this prayer?

_____
_____
_____
_____
_____
_____

God is our Example

Example: a pattern or model for others to imitate

Watch what God does, and then you do it, like children who learn proper behavior from their parents. Mostly what God does is love you. Keep company with him and learn a life of love. Observe how Christ loved us. Love like that. Ephesians 5:1-2 (MSG)

When we read about Jesus in the Bible, we see that He obeyed God and treated others kindly. He helped those who were needy. He taught them how to live so that God would be pleased. Jesus is the example that God gave us to show us more about who He is. As we learn about Jesus, we learn about God. Praise God that He gave us a perfect example.

Praise

_____
_____
_____
_____
_____
_____
_____

Repent

*If you forgive those who sin against you,
your heavenly Father will forgive you.
Matthew 6:14 (NLT)*

God is our Example

Acknowledge

_____
_____
_____
_____
_____
_____

Yield

_____
_____
_____
_____
_____

Don't let anyone think less of you because you are young. Be an
example to all believers in what you say, in the way you live,
in your love, your faith, and your purity.
1 Timothy 4:12 (NLT)

How did God respond to this prayer?

_____
_____
_____
_____
_____
_____
_____

God is Faithful

Faithful: deserving trust; showing true and constant support or loyalty; keeping your promises

For the LORD is good. His unfailing love continues forever, and his faithfulness continues to each generation. Psalm 100:5 (NLT)

We all make promises, but sometimes we don't keep those promises. When God makes a promise He always keeps it. He will never go back on His promises. God has promised to love us forever. He loves you, your parents, your grandparents and, though you might think this is a funny thought, He even loves your children and your grandchildren. Praise God that He has been faithful in the past, He is faithful now and He will be faithful in the future. Great is His faithfulness!

Praise

_____

_____

_____

_____

_____

_____

Repent

But if we confess our sins to him, he is faithful and just
to forgive us our sins and to cleanse us from all wickedness.
1 John 1:9 (NLT)

God is Faithful

Acknowledge

_____
_____
_____
_____
_____
_____

Yield

_____
_____
_____
_____
_____

He will cover you with his feathers. He will shelter you with his wings.
His faithful promises are your armor and protection.
Psalm 91:4(NLT)

How did God respond to this prayer?

_____
_____
_____
_____
_____
_____

God says, "Fear Not!"

Fear: to be afraid of something as likely to be dangerous, painful or threatening – **Or** a feeling of respect or wonder inspired by greatness; filled with awe

Don't be afraid, for I am with you. Don't be discouraged, for I am your God. I will strengthen you and help you. I will hold you up with my victorious right hand. Isaiah 41:10 (NLT)

There are two kinds of fear. One kind of fear is our reaction to something that scares us. At times we are afraid of the dark, or of taking a test, or facing a bully. A second kind of fear is used a lot in the Bible where we are told to fear God. This does not mean that we should be afraid of God, but that we should be amazed at how great He is. Because He is so great, He assures us that He is with us always. When we feel afraid, praise God, He tells us, "Fear Not!"

Praise

_____

_____

_____

_____

_____

_____

Repent

But you offer forgiveness that we might learn to fear you.
Psalm 130:4 (NLT)

God says, "Fear Not!"

Acknowledge

_____
_____
_____
_____
_____
_____

Yield

_____
_____
_____
_____
_____

This is my command—be strong and courageous! Do not be afraid or
discouraged. For the LORD your God is with you wherever you go.
Joshua 1:9 (NLT)

How did God respond to this prayer?

_____
_____
_____
_____
_____
_____

Date: _____

God Fights our Battles

Fight: to actively oppose; to struggle in order to overcome

No human wisdom or understanding or plan can stand against the
LORD. The horse is prepared for the day of battle,
but the victory belongs to the LORD.
Proverbs 21:30-31 (NLT)

Some struggles we face are very difficult. We may try hard to overcome and still feel defeated, but God cannot be defeated. When we put our trust in Him to fight our battles, He is always victorious. In the Bible there is a story about a big battle that God won, not because the soldiers fought, but because they shouted praise to God.* Praise God that He is victorious in battle! (* 2 Chronicles 20:1-30)

Praise

_____
_____
_____
_____
_____

Repent

For we are not fighting against flesh-and-blood enemies, but against
evil rulers and authorities of the unseen world, against mighty powers
in this dark world, and against evil spirits in the heavenly places.
Ephesians 6:12 (NLT)

God Fights our Battles

Acknowledge

_____
_____
_____
_____
_____
_____

Yield

_____
_____
_____
_____
_____

For the LORD your God is going with you! He will fight for you against your enemies, and he will give you victory!
Deuteronomy 20:4(NLT)

How did God respond to this prayer?

_____
_____
_____
_____
_____
_____

God Finishes

Finish: to complete; to give final touches; to bring to an end

Jesus knew that his mission was now finished, and to fulfill Scripture he said, "I am thirsty." A jar of sour wine was sitting there, so they soaked a sponge in it, put it on a hyssop branch, and held it up to his lips. When Jesus had tasted it, he said, "It is finished!" Then he bowed his head and released his spirit. John 19:28-30 (NLT)

God sent Jesus to do a job that we could not do. God wanted every person to have a relationship with Him, but our sin kept that from happening. Only if the penalty for our sin was paid could we have that relationship with God. Nothing we can do is enough to pay the penalty. God sent His Son, Jesus, who was without sin, the only One who could satisfy the justice that God required. When Jesus died on the cross, the penalty was paid in full. That is why Jesus said, "It is finished." Praise God that He finishes.

Praise

_____

_____

_____

_____

Repent

I have swept away your sins like a cloud. I have scattered your offenses like the morning mist. Oh, return to me, for I have paid the price to set you free. Isaiah 44:22 (NLT)

God Finishes

Acknowledge

_____
_____
_____
_____
_____
_____

Yield

_____
_____
_____
_____
_____

And I am certain that God, who began the good work within you, will
continue his work until it is finally finished
on the day when Christ Jesus returns.
Philippians 1:6 (NLT)

How did God respond to this prayer?

_____
_____
_____
_____
_____
_____

God Forgives

Forgive: to pardon; to give up resentment or the desire to punish; to let go of wrongs

Finally, I confessed all my sins to you and stopped trying to hide my guilt. I said to myself, "I will confess my rebellion to the LORD." And you forgave me! All my guilt is gone.
Psalm 32:5 (NLT)

One of the hardest things God asks us to do is to say, "I am sorry. Will you forgive me?" We don't like to admit that we have done wrong. But until we do, we are filled with that awful feeling of guilt. When we confess our sin and repent, that awful feeling goes away because we know that God has promised to forgive. Praise God that He forgives.

Praise

_____
_____
_____
_____
_____
_____

Repent

And I will forgive their wickedness,
and I will never again remember their sins.
Hebrews 8:12 (NLT)

God Forgives

Acknowledge

_____
_____
_____
_____
_____
_____

Yield

_____
_____
_____
_____
_____

Lᴏʀᴅ, if you kept a record of our sins, who, O Lord, could ever survive? But you offer forgiveness, that we might learn to fear you.
Psalm 130:3-4 (NLT)

How did God respond to this prayer?

_____
_____
_____
_____
_____
_____

Date: _____

God is For You

For: in your best interest; in your defense; in favor of you

This I know, that God is for me. In God, whose word I praise, In the LORD, whose word I praise. In God I have put my trust, I shall not be afraid.
Psalm 56:9b-11a (NASB)

When we watch a sporting event, often we choose a team we like and say, "I am for that team!" God has chosen you and He is "for you!" Sometimes people think of God and are afraid of Him and fear that He will do bad things to us. That is not true. The Bible shows us that God is always good. He loves us so much that He would do anything to make us happy. He only asks that we love Him and obey Him. When we do, He showers us with blessings. Oh, yes! Praise God that is for you!

Praise

_____
_____
_____
_____
_____

Repent
In the same way, there is more joy in heaven over one lost sinner who repents and returns to God than over ninety-nine others who are righteous and haven't strayed away! Luke 15:7 (NLT)

God is For You

Acknowledge

_____
_____
_____
_____
_____
_____

Yield

_____
_____
_____
_____
_____
_____

What shall we say about such wonderful things as these?
If God is for us, who can ever be against us?
Romans 8:31 (NLT)

How did God respond to this prayer?

_____
_____
_____
_____
_____
_____
_____

God is your Friend

Friend: to know someone well and to be on the same side of a struggle; not an enemy or foe; a supporter or sympathizer

There is no greater love than to lay down one's life for one's friends. You are my friends if you do what I command. Now you are my friends, since I have told you everything the Father told me.
John 15:13-14,15b (NLT)

God wants you to know that He is your friend. He wants you to talk with Him, just as you do your friends. He wants to be your closest friend. He loves you so much He was willing to lay down His life so that you could be His friend. We can be a good friend if we obey His Word and live in a way that will please Him. Praise God that He calls us "friend."

Praise

_____

_____

_____

_____

_____

_____

Repent

The LORD is a friend to those who fear him. He teaches them his covenant. My eyes are always on the LORD, for he rescues me from the traps of my enemies. Psalm 25:14-15 (NLT)

God is your Friend

Acknowledge

_____
_____
_____
_____
_____
_____

Yield

_____
_____
_____
_____
_____

There are "friends" who destroy each other,
but a real friend sticks closer than a brother.
Proverbs 18:24 (NLT)

How did God respond to this prayer?

_____
_____
_____
_____
_____
_____

Date: _____

God Gives

Give: to transfer from one's own possession to that of another; to donate

For the LORD God is our sun and our shield. He gives us grace and glory.
The LORD will withhold no good thing from those who do what is right.
Psalm 84:11 (NLT)

God gives good things. He is the source of everything. He gives us food, water, sunshine and rain. He gives us knowledge and understanding, strength and rest. He gives us hope and encouragement, wisdom and peace. He gives us victory through our Lord Jesus Christ. As you go through each day, look all around and praise God for all the ways He gives.

Praise

_____
_____
_____
_____
_____
_____

Repent

Keep watch and pray, so that you will not give in to temptation.
For the spirit is willing, but the body is weak.
Mark 14:38 (NLT)

God Gives

Acknowledge

_____
_____
_____
_____
_____
_____

Yield

_____
_____
_____
_____
_____
_____

Give, and you will receive. Your gift will return to you in full—pressed down, shaken together to make room for more, running over, and poured into your lap. The amount you give will determine the amount you get back. Luke 6:38 (NLT)

How did God respond to this prayer?

_____
_____
_____
_____
_____
_____

God is Good

Good: honorable, worthy, dependable, reliable, right, thorough, complete, sufficient

How great is the goodness you have stored up for those who fear you.
You lavish it on those who come to you for protection,
blessing them before the watching world.
Psalm 31:19 (NLT)

Some people question the goodness of God. They ask, "If God is good, why does He let bad things happen?" Just as this verse states, if we come to God for protection, He will bless us. It is when we walk away from God that we expose ourselves to trouble and harm. The Bible says that no matter what happens, God is working all things for our good. Praise God that we can trust Him, for He is good.

Praise

_____
_____
_____
_____
_____
_____

Repent

O Lord, you are so good, so ready to forgive, so full of unfailing love
for all who ask for your help.
Psalm 86:5 (NLT)

God is Good

Acknowledge

_____
_____
_____
_____
_____
_____

Yield

_____
_____
_____
_____
_____

Give thanks to the LORD, for he is good!
His faithful love endures forever.
1 Chronicles 16:34 (NLT)

How did God respond to this prayer?

_____
_____
_____
_____
_____
_____

Date: _____

God is Gracious

Gracious: merciful; compassionate; showing undeserved favor or love

*For your kingdom is an everlasting kingdom. You rule throughout all
generations. The LORD always keeps his promises;
he is gracious in all he does.
Psalm 145:13 (NLT)*

Have you ever received a gift, a compliment, and award or recognition
that you felt you did not deserve? Receiving such things can be difficult.
It is much easier to receive those things we have worked for or feel that
we deserve. Even though it is undeserved, God pours out His grace on
us. He forgives our sin and blesses us with His love. God is gracious. He
gives us what we do not deserve. Praise God that He is gracious.

Praise

_____
_____
_____
_____
_____

Repent

*Bring your confessions, and return to the LORD. Say to him,
"Forgive all our sins and graciously receive us,
so that we may offer you our praises.
Hosea 14:2 (NLT)*

God is Gracious

Acknowledge

_____
_____
_____
_____
_____
_____
_____

Yield

_____
_____
_____
_____
_____
_____

Teach me to do your will, for you are my God.
May your gracious Spirit lead me forward on a firm footing.
Psalm 143:10 (NLT)

How did God respond to this prayer?

_____
_____
_____
_____
_____
_____
_____

Date: _____

God Heals

Heal: to make well or healthy again; to restore; to free from grief, troubles or evil

O LORD, if you heal me, I will be truly healed; if you save me, I will be truly saved. My praises are for you alone!
Jeremiah 17:14 (NLT)

God designed our body in a miraculous way. When we get sick or hurt, our body can heal itself. That is God healing us. God heals us in many other ways. He heals our mind, our emotions and our spirit when we are troubled or confused. He heals relationships and misunderstandings. God heals perfectly and for that we praise Him!

Praise

_____
_____
_____
_____
_____
_____
_____

Repent

Confess your sins to each other and pray for each other
so that you may be healed.
James 5:16a (NLT)

God Heals

Acknowledge

_____
_____
_____
_____
_____
_____

Yield

_____
_____
_____
_____
_____

Don't be impressed with your own wisdom. Instead, fear the LORD and
turn away from evil. Then you will have healing for your body
and strength for your bones.
Proverbs 3:7-9 (NLT)

How did God respond to this prayer?

_____
_____
_____
_____
_____
_____

God Helps

Help: to give assistance or support; to give relief to

The LORD is my strength and shield. I trust him with all my heart.
He helps me, and my heart is filled with joy.
I burst out in songs of thanksgiving.
Psalm 28:7 (NLT)

Everyone needs help at one time or another. Often we are embarrassed to ask for help and sometimes those we ask are unable to help us. The first thing we should do when we need help is ask God in prayer, for He is always ready to help. He will give the wisdom, strength and guidance we need. He is always near. Praise God that He knows what is best and He will help in ways that will meet our needs.

Praise

_____
_____
_____
_____
_____
_____

Repent

O Lord, you are so good, so ready to forgive,
so full of unfailing love for all who ask for your help.
Psalm 86:5 (NLT)

God Helps

Acknowledge

_____
_____
_____
_____
_____
_____

Yield

_____
_____
_____
_____
_____

Commit everything you do to the LORD.
Trust him, and he will help you.
Psalm 37:5 (NLT)

How did God respond to this prayer?

_____
_____
_____
_____
_____
_____

Date: _____

God is Holy

Holy: spiritually perfect or pure; sinless; deserving praise and adoration

Who is like you among the gods, O Lord—glorious in holiness,
awesome in splendor, performing great wonders?
Exodus 15:11 (NLT)

Through the ages, mankind has worshipped all kinds of gods. Some are idols made of metal, wood or stone. Some worship money, position or pleasure as their god. But there is only one true living God. He is real, the creator of all things, not something made by human hands. God is holy. He is good and pure and perfect beyond anything we can understand. Praise God for He is holy and worthy of our worship and praise.

Praise

_____

_____

_____

_____

Repent

The high and lofty one who lives in eternity, the Holy One, says this:
"I live in the high and holy place with those whose spirits are contrite
and humble. I restore the crushed spirit of the humble
and revive the courage of those with repentant hearts.
Isaiah 57:15 (NLT)

God is Holy

Acknowledge

_____
_____
_____
_____
_____
_____

Yield

_____
_____
_____
_____
_____

Let all that I am praise the LORD; with my whole heart,
I will praise his holy name.
Psalm 103:1 (NLT)

How did God respond to this prayer?

_____
_____
_____
_____
_____
_____
_____

God is our Hope

Hope: a confident feeling of expectation and a desire for something to happen

Let all that I am wait quietly before God, for my hope is in him.
He alone is my rock and my salvation,
my fortress where I will not be shaken.
Psalm 62:5-6 (NLT)

What are some of the things you hope for? How confident are you that they will happen? There are times when we are disappointed that the things we hope for do not happen. God always wants what is best. When we put our hope in God, we are trusting His love and His faithfulness to bring about what is best. When we put our hope in God, we will not be disappointed. Praise God that He is our hope.

Praise

_____
_____
_____
_____
_____
_____

Repent

May integrity and honesty protect me, for I put my hope in you.
Psalm 25:21 (NLT)

God is our Hope

Acknowledge

_____
_____
_____
_____
_____
_____

Yield

_____
_____
_____
_____
_____

Lead me by your truth and teach me,
for you are the God who saves me.
All day long I put my hope in you.
Psalm 25:5 (NLT)

How did God respond to this prayer?

_____
_____
_____
_____
_____

God values Humility

Humility: absence of pride; not thinking you are better than other people

> *Though he was God, he did not think of equality with God as something to cling to. Instead, he gave up his divine privileges; he took the humble position of a slave and was born as a human being.*
> *Philippians 2:6-7a (NLT)*

This verse explains that God came to earth in human form as Jesus Christ. Think of it – all powerful God made himself to be just like you. He walked and talked and lived his life on earth. He willingly humbled himself because He longed to have a relationship with you. He endured temptation, suffering and death just so you could know Him. God asks to be humble rather than prideful for He values humility. Praise God that He is humble.

Praise

_____

_____

_____

Repent

> *Then if my people who are called by my name will humble themselves and pray and seek my face and turn from their wicked ways, I will hear from heaven and will forgive their sins and restore their land.*
> *2 Chronicles 7:14 (NLT)*

God values Humility

Acknowledge

_____
_____
_____
_____
_____
_____

Yield

_____
_____
_____
_____
_____

If you are wise and understand God's ways,
prove it by living an honorable life, doing good works
with the humility that comes from wisdom.
James 3:13 (NLT)

How did God respond to this prayer?

_____
_____
_____
_____
_____

God does not Hurry

Hurry: to move with haste (the act of hurrying carelessly or recklessly)
Wait: to remain in readiness or in anticipation until something happens

We wait in hope for the LORD; he is our help and our shield. In him our hearts rejoice, for we trust in his holy name. May your unfailing love be with us, LORD, even as we put our hope in you. Psalm 33:20-22 (NIV)

God does not hurry. He teaches us to wait. God is not bound by time as we are. At times we pray and want God to answer immediately, but He does not act in haste, carelessly or recklessly answering our prayers. We must learn to put our hope in Him, to trust Him and to wait – expectantly. The answer will come. It may be "yes," it may be "no," or it may be "not now – wait for My perfect answer at the perfect time." Praise God, wanting what is best for us, He does not hurry. He teaches us to wait.

Praise

_____
_____
_____
_____

Repent

*So also Christ was offered once for all time as a sacrifice to take away the sins of many people. He will come again, not to deal with our sins, but to bring salvation to all who are eagerly waiting for him.
Hebrews 9:28 (NLT)*

God does not Hurry

Acknowledge

_____
_____
_____
_____
_____
_____

Yield

_____
_____
_____
_____
_____

Yet those who wait for the LORD will gain new strength; they will mount up with wings like eagles, they will run and not get tired, they will walk and not become weary.
Isaiah 40:31 (NASB)

How did God respond to this prayer?

_____
_____
_____
_____
_____
_____

God does the Impossible

Impossible: not able to occur, exist, or be done

Jesus looked at them intently and said, "Humanly speaking, it is impossible. But not with God. Everything is possible with God."
Mark 10:27 (NLT)

Sometimes we give up because what we are trying to do or what we are hoping for seems impossible. Jesus showed us that He was able to do the impossible when He healed the eyes of the man who was born blind, when he healed the crippled man who had never walked and when he raised back to life people who had died. When things seem impossible, go to God, trust Him, believe Him and praise Him because God does the impossible!

Praise

_____

_____

_____

_____

Repent

When he sees all that is accomplished by his anguish, he will be satisfied. And because of his experience, my righteous servant will make it possible for many to be counted righteous, for he will bear all their sins.
Isaiah 53:11(NLT)

God does the Impossible

Acknowledge

_____
_____
_____
_____
_____
_____

Yield

_____
_____
_____
_____
_____

Then the name of our Lord Jesus will be honored because of the way you live, and you will be honored along with him. This is all made possible because of the grace of our God and Lord, Jesus Christ.
2 Thessalonians 1:12 (NLT)

How did God respond to this prayer?

_____
_____
_____
_____

God Intercedes

Intercede: to pray, plead or make a request on behalf of another

And the Holy Spirit helps us in our weakness. For example, we don't know what God wants us to pray for. But the Holy Spirit prays for us with groanings that cannot be expressed in words. And the Father who knows all hearts knows what the Spirit is saying, for the Spirit pleads for us believers in harmony with God's own will.
Romans 8:26-27(NLT)

At times when we need help, we try to talk to God in prayer, but we just don't know what to say. God tells us in the Bible that His Spirit, the Holy Spirit, knows how to pray for us and will pray, asking God to help us in a way that will bring Him glory. It is comforting to know that God loves us so much that He prays for us. Praise God that He intercedes.

Praise

_____
_____
_____
_____
_____
_____

Repent

He bore the sins of many and interceded for rebels.
Isaiah 53:12b (NLT)

God Intercedes

Acknowledge

_____
_____
_____
_____
_____
_____

Yield

_____
_____
_____
_____
_____

I urge you, first of all, to pray for all people. Ask God to help them;
intercede on their behalf, and give thanks for them.
1 Timothy 2:1 (NLT)

How did God respond to this prayer?

_____
_____
_____
_____
_____
_____

Date: _____

God is our Joy

Joy: a feeling of great pleasure or happiness deep within

I have loved you even as the Father has loved me. Remain in my
love. When you obey my commandments, you remain in my love, just
as I obey my Father's commandments and remain in his love. I have
told you these things so that you will be filled with my joy.
Yes, your joy will overflow!
John 15:9-11 (NLT)

Is it possible to have joy even when circumstances are difficult? When
we understand how much God loves us and that He never leaves or
forsakes us, it is possible! True joy is not based on who we are, where we
are or what we are. It is based on the fact that we belong to God who
loves us, guides us, protects us and blesses us when we follow Him in
obedience. Praise God that He is our joy.

Praise

_____

_____

_____

_____

_____

Repent

Oh, what joy for those whose disobedience is forgiven,
whose sin is put out of sight! Psalm 32:1 (NLT)

God is our Joy

Acknowledge

_____
_____
_____
_____
_____
_____

Yield

_____
_____
_____
_____
_____
_____

But let all who take refuge in you rejoice; let them sing joyful praises forever. Spread your protection over them, that all who love your name may be filled with joy.
Psalm 5:11 (NLT)

How did God respond to this prayer?

_____
_____
_____
_____
_____
_____

God is our Judge

Judge: one who makes a decision about a question after considering the evidence

But the LORD reigns forever, executing judgment from his throne. He will judge the world with justice and rule the nations with fairness.
Psalms 9:7-8 (NLT)

The Bible tells us that everyone will stand before God one day and He will judge us according to how we lived our lives. God asks us to obey Him and love others as He loves us. If we live in this way God will reward us not only now but also when we stand before Him on the Day of Judgment. Praise God that He is the righteous judge.

Praise

_____
_____
_____
_____
_____
_____

Repent

Therefore, I will judge each of you...according to your actions,
says the Sovereign LORD. Repent, and turn from your sins.
Don't let them destroy you!
Ezekiel 18:30 (NLT)

God is our Judge

Acknowledge

_____
_____
_____
_____
_____
_____

Yield

_____
_____
_____
_____
_____

And remember that the heavenly Father to whom you pray has no favorites. He will judge or reward you according to what you do. So you must live in reverent fear of him during your time here as "temporary residents." 1 Peter 1:17 (NLT)

How did God respond to this prayer?

_____
_____
_____
_____
_____
_____

God is Kind

Kind: having a friendly nature; tenderhearted; sympathetic; generous

So we praise God for the glorious grace he has poured out on us who belong to his dear Son. He is so rich in kindness and grace that he purchased our freedom with the blood of his Son and forgave our sins. He has showered his kindness on us, along with all wisdom and understanding. Ephesians 1:6-9 (NLT)

The kindness of God is shown in the life of Jesus. He expressed His kindness as he healed the sick, comforted and encouraged those who were discouraged, welcomed little children and fed the hungry. His life is our example to be kind to one another. Even a simple word of encouragement can make a big difference, just as God's kindness makes a difference in our life. Praise God that He is kind.

Praise

_____

_____

_____

_____

Repent

Get rid of all bitterness, rage, anger, harsh words, and slander, as well as all types of evil behavior. Instead, be kind to each other, tenderhearted, forgiving one another, just as God through Christ has forgiven you. Ephesians 4:31-32 (NLT)

God is Kind

Acknowledge

_____
_____
_____
_____
_____
_____

Yield

_____
_____
_____
_____
_____
_____

This is what the LORD of Heaven's Armies says:
Judge fairly, and show mercy and kindness to one another.
Zechariah 7:9 (NLT)

How did God respond to this prayer?

_____
_____
_____
_____
_____
_____
_____

God Knows

Know: to have developed a relationship with someone; to be aware through observation, inquiry, or information

O LORD, you have examined my heart and know everything about me. You know when I sit down or stand up. You know my thoughts even when I am far away. You know everything I do. You know what I am going to say even before I say it, LORD. Such knowledge is too wonderful for me, too great for me to understand!
Psalm 139:1-3b,4,6 (NLT)

Nothing is hidden from God. He sees our actions, He hears our words and He knows our thoughts. He knows everything about us because He designed us to be unique, unlike anyone else. God wants us to know Him as well as He knows us. Praise God that He knows.

Praise

_____
_____
_____
_____

Repent

But God's truth stands firm like a foundation stone with this inscription: "The LORD knows those who are his," and "All who belong to the LORD must turn away from evil."
2 Timothy 2:19 (NLT)

God Knows

Acknowledge

_____
_____
_____
_____
_____
_____

Yield

_____
_____
_____
_____
_____

_Our actions will show that we belong to the truth, so we will be
confident when we stand before God. Even if we feel guilty, God is
greater than our feelings, and he knows everything._
1 John 3:19-21 (NLT)

How did God respond to this prayer?

_____
_____
_____
_____
_____

God Leads

Lead: to guide by direction or example; to go first

*You go before me and follow me. You place your hand of blessing on
my head. Such knowledge is too wonderful for me,
too great for me to understand!*
Psalm 139:5-6 (NLT)

There are times when we are faced with difficult decisions and we don't
know where to go or what to do. Not only in those times, but in all times,
when we put our trust in God and live in obedience to His Word, He will
lead us in our thoughts and in our steps. His word in the Bible teaches us,
His Spirit guides us, and His love surrounds us. God goes first and we can
trust Him to lead us to peace and safety. Praise God that He leads.

Praise

_____
_____
_____
_____
_____
_____

Repent

*The LORD leads with unfailing love and faithfulness all who keep his
covenant and obey his demands. For the honor of your name, O LORD,
forgive my many, many sins.*
Psalm 25:10-11 (NLT)

God Leads

Acknowledge

_____
_____
_____
_____
_____
_____
_____

Yield

_____
_____
_____
_____
_____

Show me the right path, O LORD; point out the road for me to follow. Lead me by your truth and teach me, for you are the God who saves me. All day long I put my hope in you. Psalm 25:4-5 (NLT)

How did God respond to this prayer?

_____
_____
_____
_____
_____
_____

God Listens

Listen: to hear something with thoughtful attention

The LORD is close to all who call on him, yes, to all who call on him in truth. He grants the desires of those who fear him; he hears their cries for help and rescues them.
Psalm 145:18-19 (NLT)

God does not just "hear" our prayers, He "listens." He considers everything we pray about then carefully decides how to act in answer to our prayers. Just as Jesus asked the blind man, "What do you want me to do?" God wants us to ask Him specifically so that He can answer specifically. God will answer our prayers in His perfect timing and in a way that will bring Him glory. He wants us to ask and know that He is listening. He is paying careful attention to our needs. Praise God that He listens.

Praise

_____

_____

_____

_____

_____

Repent

If I had not confessed the sin in my heart, the Lord would not have listened. But God did listen! He paid attention to my prayer.
Psalm 66:18-19 (NLT)

God Listens

Acknowledge

_____
_____
_____
_____
_____
_____

Yield

_____
_____
_____
_____
_____

Listen to my voice in the morning, LORD.
Each morning I bring my requests to you and wait expectantly.
Psalm 5:3 (NLT)

How did God respond to this prayer?

_____
_____
_____
_____
_____
_____

Date: _____

God is Love

Love: a deep tender feeling of affection or devotion; putting another's needs before your own

For this is how God loved the world: He gave his one and only Son, so that everyone who believes in him will not perish but have eternal life.
John 3:16 (NLT)

God's love is accessible, it is boundless, it is compassionate, it defends. God's love encourages, it is faithful, it is full of grace and it heals. God's love is impartial, it brings joy, it knows all and it leads. God's love is merciful, it is always near, it overcomes, it is patient. God's love quiets the troubled soul, it restores and it saves. God's love transforms, it is unfailing, it is victorious and it is wise. God's love sees all, like an X-ray. It does not yield to the enemy and God is zealous to let us know how much he loves us. Even using every letter of the alphabet is not sufficient to describe God's love for us. Praise God that He is love.

Praise

_____

_____

_____

_____

_____

Repent

This is real love—not that we loved God, but that he loved us and sent his Son as a sacrifice to take away our sins.1 John 4:10 (NLT)

God is Love

Acknowledge

_____
_____
_____
_____
_____
_____

Yield

_____
_____
_____
_____
_____

Dear friends, let us continue to love one another, for love comes from God. Anyone who loves is a child of God and knows God. But anyone who does not love does not know God, for God is love.
1 John 4:7-8 (NLT)

How did God respond to this prayer?

_____
_____
_____
_____
_____

God is Merciful

Merciful: forgiving; compassionate; not giving a punishment that is deserved

But you, O Lord, are a God of compassion and mercy, slow to get angry and filled with unfailing love and faithfulness.
Psalm 86:15 (NLT)

There are two words that are important to know and understand. One is "mercy" which refers to "not getting what we deserve." We deserve to be punished for our sins, but because Jesus took the punishment for us on the cross, we don't get the punishment we deserve. The second word is "grace" which means "getting what we don't deserve." Because of God's love and grace, even though we don't deserve it, God forgives our sin and gives us a home with Him in heaven. Praise God that He is merciful and He does not require that we pay the penalty for sin.

Praise

_____

_____

_____

_____

Repent

People who conceal their sins will not prosper, but if they confess and turn from them, they will receive mercy.
Proverbs 28:13 (NLT)

God is Merciful

Acknowledge

_____
_____
_____
_____
_____
_____

Yield

_____
_____
_____
_____
_____

No, O people, the LORD has told you what is good, and this is what he
requires of you: to do what is right, to love mercy,
and to walk humbly with your God.
Micah 6:8 (NLT)

How did God respond to this prayer?

_____
_____
_____
_____
_____

God is Mighty

Mighty: remarkably great power or force; great or superior strength

...O Lᴏʀᴅ, God of our ancestors, you alone are the God who is in heaven. You are ruler of all the kingdoms of the earth. You are powerful and mighty; no one can stand against you!
2 Chronicles 20:6 (NLT)

"My God is so big, so strong and so mighty, there's nothing my God cannot do." You may remember singing this song. It is a great reminder that God is greater than anything and everything. We face an enemy, Satan, who tries to lure us into things that will harm us, but God will fight for us with His mighty weapons and He is always victorious! Remember, nothing is impossible with God. Praise God for He is mighty!

Praise

_____
_____
_____
_____
_____

Repent

The Son radiates God's own glory and expresses the very character of God, and he sustains everything by the mighty power of his command. When he had cleansed us from our sins, he sat down in the place of honor at the right hand of the majestic God in heaven.
Hebrews 1:3 (NLT)

God is Mighty

Acknowledge

_____
_____
_____
_____
_____
_____

Yield

_____
_____
_____
_____
_____

*Now all glory to God, who is able, through his mighty power at work
within us, to accomplish infinitely more than we might ask or think.
Ephesians 3:20 (NLT)*

How did God respond to this prayer?

_____
_____
_____
_____
_____
_____

God is Near

Near: close by

The LORD is near to all who call on him, to all who call on him in truth.
Psalm 145:18 (NIV)

"Omnipresent" is a big word you might hear that means God is everywhere at the same time. You and I can only be in one place at a time, but God is so much greater. When we call out to Him, He hears us because He is always near. He is near in the morning and when we sleep at night. He is near you and He is near everyone. He surrounds us and the generations to come with all that He is – protection, provision, wisdom, joy, peace, comfort, and on and on. Praise God for even right now, God is near - everywhere!

Praise

_____
_____
_____
_____
_____
_____
_____

Repent

From then on Jesus began to preach, "Repent of your sins and turn to God, for the Kingdom of Heaven is near."
Matthew 4:17 (NLT)

God is Near

Acknowledge

_____
_____
_____
_____
_____
_____

Yield

_____
_____
_____
_____
_____

But as for me, how good it is to be near God!
I have made the Sovereign LORD my shelter,
and I will tell everyone about the wonderful things you do.
Psalm 73:28 (NLT)

How did God respond to this prayer?

_____
_____
_____
_____
_____

God makes things New

New: coming into being for the first time; different from that which has been before

This means that anyone who belongs to Christ has become a new person. The old life is gone; a new life has begun!
2 Corinthians 5:17(NLT)

Although there are times when we take something old and try to fix it, spruce it up, or make it better, we cannot take something old and make it new. Yet, that is what God does in so many ways. When we ask Jesus to be our Lord and Savior He takes away our sin and gives us a new spirit, a new attitude, and a new life. He replaces the old with the new. Praise God that He is able to make things new!

Praise

_____
_____
_____
_____
_____

Repent

And I will give you a new heart, and I will put a new spirit in you. I will take out your stony, stubborn heart and give you a tender, responsive heart. And I will put my Spirit in you so that you will follow my decrees and be careful to obey my regulations.
Ezekiel 36:26-27 (NLT)

God makes things New

Acknowledge

_____
_____
_____
_____
_____
_____

Yield

_____
_____
_____
_____
_____

He has given me a new song to sing, a hymn of praise to our God.
Many will see what he has done and be amazed.
They will put their trust in the LORD.
Psalm 40:3 (NLT)

How did God respond to this prayer?

_____
_____
_____
_____
_____

Date: _____

God is Patient

Patient: able to remain calm and not become annoyed when waiting for a long time or when dealing with difficulties

The Lord isn't really being slow about his promise, as some people think. No, he is being patient for your sake. He does not want anyone to be destroyed, but wants everyone to repent.
2 Peter 3:9 (NLT)

It is easy to become annoyed when we have to wait for someone or for something to go our way. At times this can stir up anger inside. When this happens it helps to focus on God who is patient and loving. God wants us to be patient and loving to others just as He is to us. He wants to have a relationship with us and He calmly waits for us to trust Him, all the while showing us His love. Praise God that He is patient!

Praise

_____

_____

_____

_____

Repent

Don't you see how wonderfully kind, tolerant, and patient God is with you? Does this mean nothing to you? Can't you see that his kindness is intended to turn you from your sin?
Romans 2:4 (NLT)

God is Patient

Acknowledge

_____
_____
_____
_____
_____
_____

Yield

_____
_____
_____
_____
_____

Since God chose you to be the holy people he loves, you must clothe yourselves with tenderhearted mercy, kindness, humility, gentleness, and patience. Make allowance for each other's faults, and forgive anyone who offends you. Remember, the Lord forgave you, so you must forgive others. Colossians 3:12-13 (NLT)

How did God respond to this prayer?

_____
_____
_____
_____
_____

Date: _____

God is Peace

Peace: a state of calm; freedom from strife or discord; rest of heart, mind and spirit

You will keep in perfect peace all who trust in you,
all whose thoughts are fixed (focused) on you!
Isaiah 26:3 (NLT)

Our minds are filled with all kinds of thoughts throughout the day. Some thoughts make us happy and other thoughts make us sad. Some thoughts are restful and others stir us up. No matter what we experience throughout each day, we must remember that God is with us, that He loves us, and He watches over us. When we focus our thoughts on who God is, even when we face difficulties, we find peace - a gift that is beyond our ability to understand. Praise God that He is our peace.

Praise

_____

_____

_____

_____

_____

Repent

So letting your sinful nature control your mind leads to death. But
letting the Spirit control your mind leads to life and peace.
Romans 8:6 (NLT)

God is Peace

Acknowledge

_____
_____
_____
_____
_____
_____

Yield

_____
_____
_____
_____
_____

Jesus said, "I am leaving you with a gift—peace of mind and heart.
And the peace I give is a gift the world cannot give.
So don't be troubled or afraid."
John 14:27 (NLT)

How did God respond to this prayer?

_____
_____
_____
_____
_____

God is Perfect

Perfect: flawless; free from faults or defects; completely correct; lacking nothing

He is the Rock; his deeds are perfect. Everything he does is just and fair. He is a faithful God who does no wrong;
how just and upright he is!
Deuteronomy 32:4 (NLT)

Although we use the word "perfect" to describe many things, it would be very difficult to find something that is truly perfect. There could be no defects or flaws. If it were a person, they could have no faults. How hard would it be to find that! It is almost impossible to really understand the fullness of God. He is the picture of perfection for He is free from faults, completely correct and lacks nothing. Praise God – He is perfect!

Praise

_____

_____

_____

_____

_____

Repent

Just think how much more the blood of Christ will purify our consciences from sinful deeds so that we can worship the living God. For by the power of the eternal Spirit, Christ offered himself to God as a perfect sacrifice for our sins. Hebrews 9:14 (NLT)

God is Perfect

Acknowledge

_____
_____
_____
_____
_____
_____

Yield

_____
_____
_____
_____
_____

Don't copy the behavior and customs of this world, but let God transform you into a new person by changing the way you think. Then you will learn to know God's will for you, which is good and pleasing and perfect. Romans 12:2 (NLT)

How did God respond to this prayer?

_____
_____
_____
_____
_____

God is Personal

Personal: related to or affecting a particular person; to be intimately familiar with

You saw me before I was born. Every day of my life was recorded in your book. Every moment was laid out before a single day had passed.
Psalm 139:16 (NLT)

What an amazing thought that God personally knows every person that ever existed or that ever will exist. God is our creator and the Bible tells us that He even knows the number of hairs on our head. God watches over us, provides ways for us to resist temptation, guides us and protects us. He hears our every prayer and has plans for us that give us hope and a future. Praise God that He knows us personally!

Praise

_____
_____
_____
_____
_____
_____
_____
_____
_____

Repent

Yes, each of us will give a personal account to God.
Romans 14:12 (NLT)

God is Personal

Acknowledge

_____
_____
_____
_____
_____
_____

Yield

_____
_____
_____
_____
_____

Do not be afraid or discouraged, for the LORD will personally go ahead
of you. He will be with you; he will neither fail you nor abandon you.
Deuteronomy 31:8 (NLT)

How did God respond to this prayer?

_____
_____
_____
_____
_____
_____

God Protects

Protect: to keep safe from harm or injury; to defend or guard from attack

He grants a treasure of common sense to the honest. He is a shield to those who walk with integrity. He guards the paths of the just and protects those who are faithful to him. Proverbs 2:7-8 (NLT)

There is no power greater than God. He is able to protect you in every way. He protects you from harm as he watches over you. The Bible tells us that He orders His angels to protect you wherever you go. He also protects us from the attacks of Satan. This enemy of God tries in many ways to harm us, but God rescues us and wins the victory. Praise God that He protects!

Praise

_____
_____
_____
_____
_____

Repent

Gather before judgment begins, before your time to repent is blown away like chaff. Seek to do what is right and to live humbly. Perhaps even yet the LORD will protect you—protect you from his anger on that day of destruction. Zephaniah 2:2a,3b (NLT)

God Protects

Acknowledge

_____
_____
_____
_____
_____
_____

Yield

_____
_____
_____
_____
_____

May the LORD bless you and protect you.
May the LORD smile on you and be gracious to you.
Numbers 6:24-25 (NLT)

How did God respond to this prayer?

_____
_____
_____
_____
_____
_____

God Plans

Plan: a set of actions that have been thought of as a way to do or achieve something

O LORD my God, you have performed many wonders for us. Your plans for us are too numerous to list. You have no equal. If I tried to recite all your wonderful deeds, I would never come to the end of them.
Psalm 40:5 (NLT)

Some believe that the world is just a lot of random things that come about spontaneously. The chances are impossible that the universe, the earth, our bodies, and all of creation "just happened" so perfectly. All of creation points to a creator who has knowledge beyond anything we can understand. His plans are perfect and He has a plan for your life. Praise God that the plans He has established for you are good.

Praise

_____
_____
_____
_____
_____
_____
_____

Repent

Jesus gave his life for our sins, just as God our Father planned, in order to rescue us from this evil world in which we live.
Galatians 1:4 (NLT)

God Plans

Acknowledge

_____
_____
_____
_____
_____
_____

Yield

_____
_____
_____
_____
_____

For I know the plans I have for you," says the LORD. "They are plans for good and not for disaster, to give you a future and a hope.
Jeremiah 29:11 (NLT)

How did God respond to this prayer?

_____
_____
_____
_____
_____
_____
_____

God is Powerful

Powerful: a person or thing having great ability to make things happen

(God said,) "My grace is all you need. My power works best in
weakness." So now I am glad to boast about my weaknesses,
so that the power of Christ can work through me.
2 Corinthians 12:9 (NLT)

This verse may seem hard to understand, but God was telling the apostle Paul that he didn't need to depend on his own strength to do the work God had planned for him. He needed to depend on God's power, which is greater than any human power. There are times when we feel that we are weak. That is when we need to shift our focus from what we can do to what God can do. Praise God that we can do all things when we trust in powerful God.

Praise

_____
_____
_____
_____
_____

Repent

For by the power of the eternal Spirit,
Christ offered himself to God as a perfect sacrifice for our sins.
Hebrews 9:14b (NLT)

God is Powerful

Acknowledge

_____
_____
_____
_____
_____
_____

Yield

_____
_____
_____
_____
_____

Praise the LORD, all you nations. Praise him, all you people of the earth. For his unfailing love for us is powerful; the LORD's faithfulness endures forever. Praise the LORD!
Psalm 117:1-2 (NLT)

How did God respond to this prayer?

_____
_____
_____
_____
_____
_____

God is our Provider

Provide: to get ready beforehand; to supply

Isaac turned to Abraham and said, "Father?" "Yes, my son?" Abraham replied. "We have the fire and the wood," the boy said, "but where is the sheep for the burnt offering?" "God will provide a sheep for the burnt offering, my son," Abraham answered. And they both walked on together. When they arrived at the place where God had told him to go, Abraham built an altar and arranged the wood on it. Then he tied his son, Isaac, and laid him on the altar on top of the wood. Then Abraham looked up and saw a ram caught by its horns in a thicket. So he took the ram and sacrificed it as a burnt offering in place of his son. Abraham named the place Yahweh-Yireh (which means "the LORD will provide"). To this day, people still use that name as a proverb: "On the mountain of the LORD it will be provided." Genesis 22:7-14 (NLT)

God asked Abraham to do the unthinkable. How difficult it must have been to place his son on the altar of sacrifice. But even as he did, Abraham was trusting God to provide the ram so that his son would be saved. God provided. Praise God that He provides all that we need.

Praise

_____

_____

Repent

You do not desire a sacrifice, or I would offer one. You do not want a burnt offering. The sacrifice you desire is a broken spirit. You will not reject a broken and repentant heart, O God. Psalm 51:15-17 (NLT)

116

God is our Provider

Acknowledge

_____
_____
_____
_____
_____
_____

Yield

_____
_____
_____
_____
_____

And this same God who takes care of me will supply all your needs from his glorious riches, which have been given to us in Christ Jesus.
Philippians 4:19 (NLT)

How did God respond to this prayer?

_____
_____
_____
_____
_____
_____
_____

Date: _____

God Quiets

Quiet: absence of noise; to make or become silent, calm or still

Let all that I am wait quietly before God, for my hope is in him.
He alone is my rock and my salvation,
my fortress where I will not be shaken.
Psalm 62:5-6 (NLT)

Often we fill our day with noises that occupy our thoughts. It is good to be quiet and listen. The Spirit of God speaks to our hearts in those quiet times. It is during those quiet times that we can focus on who God is. Knowing that God loves us and is always near gives us a sense of security and calm. God asks us to quietly wait and trust Him to be our help in times of need. Praise God! Because He quiets us, nothing can shake us up.

Praise

_____

_____

_____

_____

_____

Repent
He was oppressed and treated harshly, yet he never said a word.
Unjustly condemned, he was led away.... my righteous servant will
make it possible for many to be counted righteous,
for he will bear all their sins. Isaiah 53:7,8a,11b

118

God Quiets

Acknowledge

_____
_____
_____
_____
_____
_____

Yield

_____
_____
_____
_____
_____

*The LORD your God in your midst, The Mighty One, will save; He will
rejoice over you with gladness, He will quiet you with His love,
He will rejoice over you with singing.*
Zephaniah 3:17 (NKJV)

How did God respond to this prayer?

_____
_____
_____
_____
_____
_____

God Redeems

Redeem: to buy back; repurchase; to rescue with a ransom

This is what the LORD says—your Redeemer, the Holy One of Israel:
"I am the LORD your God, who teaches you what is good for you and
leads you along the paths you should follow."
Isaiah 48:17 (NLT)

How would you feel if something was stolen from you and to get it back you had to pay for it? That is what God did. He created man so that He could have a relationship with him, but Satan stole that relationship through lies and deception. When Adam and Eve believed the lies and disobeyed God, their relationship was destroyed. In order to gain that relationship back, God had to pay a great price. His Son, Jesus, died on the cross to pay the ransom for sin. Praise God, He loves us so much He is willing to redeem us so that we can enjoy a relationship with Him.

Praise

_____
_____
_____
_____

Repent

I have swept away your sins like a cloud. I have scattered your offenses
like the morning mist. Oh, return to me, for I have paid the price
to set you free. Isaiah 44:22 (NLT)

God Redeems

Acknowledge

_____
_____
_____
_____
_____
_____

Yield

_____
_____
_____
_____
_____

May the words of my mouth and the meditation of my heart be
pleasing to you, O LORD, my rock and my redeemer.
Psalm 19:14 (NLT)

How did God respond to this prayer?

_____
_____
_____
_____
_____
_____
_____

Date: _____

God Rescues

Rescue: to free or save from danger

The LORD says, "I will rescue those who love me. I will protect those who trust in my name. When they call on me, I will answer; I will be with them in trouble. I will rescue and honor them."
Psalm 91:14-15 (NLT)

Even when we try to remain obedient to God, there are times when we find ourselves in trouble. Often when we try to make things right, our troubles get worse. It is good to ask God first to rescue and help for He knows best how to defeat the enemy. Praise God that when we are trapped in trouble, He rescues!

Praise

_____
_____
_____
_____
_____
_____
_____
_____

Repent

Jesus gave his life for our sins, just as God our Father planned, in order to rescue us from this evil world in which we live.
Galatians 1:4 (NLT)

122

God Rescues

Acknowledge

_____

_____

_____

_____

_____

_____

Yield

_____

_____

_____

_____

_____

The LORD is a friend to those who fear him.
He teaches them his covenant. My eyes are always on the LORD,
for he rescues me from the traps of my enemies.
Psalm 25:14-16 (NLT)

How did God respond to this prayer?

_____

_____

_____

_____

_____

_____

God gives Rest

Rest: freedom from activity or labor; peace of mind or spirit

Then Jesus said, "Come to me, all of you who are weary and carry heavy burdens, and I will give you rest. Take my yoke upon you. Let me teach you, because I am humble and gentle at heart, and you will find rest for your souls. For my yoke is easy to bear, and the burden I give you is light." Matthew 11:28-30 (NLT)

The definition above describes two kinds of rest. God created our bodies with a need to rest. In the account of creation we read that God rested on the seventh day. God does not tire, so He does not need to rest, but He set an example to show that we need to rest. He even included the importance of rest in the Ten Commandments. The second kind of rest is described as peace of mind or spirit. This is the rest Jesus offers when He says, "Come to me...and I will give you rest." God knows our need for both kinds of rest. Praise God, He gives rest.

Praise

_____
_____
_____
_____

Repent
So let us do our best to enter that rest. But if we disobey God, as the people of Israel did, we will fall. Hebrews 4:11 (NLT)

God gives Rest

Acknowledge

_____

_____

_____

_____

_____

_____

Yield

_____

_____

_____

_____

_____

I will bless the LORD who guides me; even at night my heart instructs
me. I know the LORD is always with me. I will not be shaken, for he is
right beside me. No wonder my heart is glad, and I rejoice.
My body rests in safety.
Psalm 16:7-9 (NLT)

How did God respond to this prayer?

_____

_____

_____

_____

_____

God is Resolute

Resolute: having or showing a lot of determination; having a fixed, firm purpose; unwavering; faithful

The LORD says, "I will rescue those who love me. I will protect those who trust in my name. When they call on me, I will answer; I will be with them in trouble. I will rescue and honor them. I will reward them with a long life and give them my salvation." Psalm 91:14-16 (NLT)

At the beginning of a new year, often we make resolutions. We say, "I will _____," and we fill in the blank. All too often the resolutions are forgotten as quickly as they are made. Our problem is we are not resolute. We lack the unwavering determination to keep our resolutions. The Scriptures are filled with resolutions that God has made to His children. When God says, "I will," He does. He resolves to keep His covenant of love and all that such a covenant encompasses - protection, salvation, forgiveness, faithfulness, rest, guidance and peace. God's fixed, firm purpose is to fill our lives with His fullness. Praise God for He is resolute.

Praise

_____

_____

Repent

"Come now, let's settle this," says the LORD. "Though your sins are like scarlet, I will make them as white as snow. Though they are red like crimson, I will make them as white as wool." Isaiah 1:18 (NLT)

126

God is Resolute

Acknowledge

_____
_____
_____
_____
_____
_____
_____

Yield

_____
_____
_____
_____
_____
_____

The LORD says, "I will guide you along the best pathway for your life.
I will advise you, and watch over you."
Psalm 32:8 (NLT)

How did God respond to this prayer?

_____
_____
_____
_____
_____
_____
_____

Date: _____

God Responds

Respond: to answer or act when called upon; to reply

The LORD says, "I was ready to respond, but no one asked for help. I was ready to be found, but no one was looking for me. I said, 'Here I am, here I am!' to a nation that did not call on my name."
Isaiah 65:1(NLT)

If you needed help in some way, wouldn't you call out and ask someone to help you? God wants to help us but He cannot respond if we do not ask. When we pray, asking for God's help, He is ready to answer and respond to our prayer in ways that are best. Throughout the scriptures there are examples of how God responds when we call upon Him. Praise God, when we call out to Him in prayer, He responds with an answer or an action that will bring Him glory.

Praise

_____
_____
_____
_____
_____

Repent
Hear me as I pray, O LORD. Be merciful and answer me!
My heart has heard you say, "Come and talk with me."
And my heart responds, "LORD, I am coming."
Psalms 27:7-8 (NLT)

128

God Responds

Acknowledge

_____
_____
_____
_____
_____
_____
_____

Yield

_____
_____
_____
_____
_____
_____

Oh, that we might know the LORD! Let us press on to know him.
He will respond to us as surely as the arrival of dawn
or the coming of rains in early spring.
Hosea 6:3 (NLT)

How did God respond to this prayer?

_____
_____
_____
_____
_____
_____
_____

God Reveals

Reveal: to make something known that was concealed or secret; to open up to view

At that time Jesus prayed this prayer: "O Father, Lord of heaven and earth, thank you for hiding these things from those who think themselves wise and clever, and for revealing them to the childlike. Yes, Father, it pleased you to do it this way!
Matthew 11:25-26 (NLT)

It seems the older we become the harder we try to figure out why God loves us as He does. Little children have a special understanding of God's love not questioning why He loves us. God wanted us to receive His love from the moment He created man. When Jesus prayed this prayer, He was thankful that God made His love so simple to understand that even little children accept it without hesitation. Praise God that He sent Jesus to reveal how much God loves us.

Praise

_____

_____

Repent

...when God our Savior revealed his kindness and love, he saved us, not because of the righteous things we had done, but because of his mercy. He washed away our sins, giving us a new birth and new life through the Holy Spirit. Titus 3:4-5 (NLT)

God Reveals

Acknowledge

_____
_____
_____
_____
_____
_____

Yield

_____
_____
_____
_____
_____
_____

For the LORD is the one who shaped the mountains, stirs up the winds, and reveals his thoughts to mankind. He turns the light of dawn into darkness and treads on the heights of the earth. The LORD God of Heaven's Armies is his name!
Amos 4:13 (NLT)

How did God respond to this prayer?

_____
_____
_____
_____
_____

God Rewards

Reward: something given to compensate for good or sometimes for evil

The laws of the LORD are true; each one is fair. They are more desirable than gold, even the finest gold. They are sweeter than honey, even honey dripping from the comb. They are a warning to your servant, a great reward for those who obey them.
Psalm 19:9b-11 (NLT)

Usually a reward is thought of as something good – something we desire. The Bible tells us that God rewards both good and evil. God promises blessing and desirable rewards for those who obey Him, but for those who choose to do evil, their reward is not anything you would ever want. So we can receive the good reward, God gives us guidance in His word. Praise God that when we trust Him and obey His guidance, we are promised to be rewarded in amazing ways that only God can give.

Praise

_____

_____

_____

_____

_____

Repent

But I, the LORD, search all hearts and examine secret motives. I give all people their due rewards, according to what their actions deserve.
Jeremiah 17:10 (NLT)

God Rewards

Acknowledge

_____
_____
_____
_____
_____
_____

Yield

_____
_____
_____
_____
_____

And it is impossible to please God without faith.
Anyone who wants to come to him must believe that God exists
and that he rewards those who sincerely seek him.
Hebrews 11:6 (NLT)

How did God respond to this prayer?

_____
_____
_____
_____
_____
_____

God is Righteous

Righteous: doing what is right; morally right; fair and just

Your righteousness, O God, reaches to the highest heavens. You have done such wonderful things. Who can compare with you, O God?
Psalm 71:19 (NLT)

Imagine how difficult it would be to keep every promise, to always tell the truth, to always be fair and do what is right even when those around you are acting wickedly. That describes God who is righteous in all ways and at all times. It is impossible to imagine how high the heavens are, just as it is impossible to comprehend the righteousness of God. Praise God that although we have sinned, when we ask Jesus to be our Savior and Lord, God gives us His righteousness.

Praise

_____
_____
_____
_____
_____
_____

Repent

But people are counted as righteous, not because of their work, but because of their faith in God who forgives sinners.
Romans 4:5 (NLT)

God is Righteous

Acknowledge

_____
_____
_____
_____
_____
_____

Yield

_____
_____
_____
_____
_____

Run from anything that stimulates youthful lusts. Instead, pursue
righteous living, faithfulness, love, and peace. Enjoy the
companionship of those who call on the Lord with pure hearts.
2 Timothy 2:22 (NLT)

How did God respond to this prayer?

_____
_____
_____
_____
_____
_____

Date: _____

God is Sacrificial

Sacrificial: to give up something at less than its value; to act on the behalf of another at great cost

For God presented Jesus as the sacrifice for sin.
People are made right with God when they believe
that Jesus sacrificed his life, shedding his blood.
Romans 3:25a (NLT)

Think of the most valuable, most precious, most dearly treasured possession you have. Now think how it would feel to have to give that to someone who did not appreciate it or deserve it. Would it be difficult to give it up? That is what God did when He gave His Son, Jesus, to pay the penalty for our sin. If God was not willing to make that sacrifice, if Jesus was not willing to sacrifice His life, we would not have the opportunity to have a relationship with God. Praise God that He is sacrificial.

Praise

_____
_____
_____
_____
_____

Repent

This is real love—not that we loved God, but that he loved us and sent
his Son as a sacrifice to take away our sins. 1 John 4:10 (NLT)

136

God is Sacrificial

Acknowledge

_____
_____
_____
_____
_____
_____

Yield

_____
_____
_____
_____
_____

Imitate God, therefore, in everything you do, because you are his dear children. Live a life filled with love, following the example of Christ. He loved us and offered himself as a sacrifice for us, a pleasing aroma to God. Ephesians 5:1-2 (NLT)

How did God respond to this prayer?

_____
_____
_____
_____
_____
_____

Date: _____

God Saves

Save: to rescue from harm or danger; to deliver from sin and punishment

God saved you by his grace when you believed. And you can't take credit for this; it is a gift from God. Salvation is not a reward for the good things we have done, so none of us can boast about it.
Ephesians 2:8-9 (NLT)

When God saves us from the penalty of sin, it is a gift. We cannot work for it and we do not deserve it; we can only receive it. When we acknowledge our sin and invite Jesus to be our Savior, God welcomes us into His family and we receive the gift of eternal life in Heaven. He continually watches over us and has the power to save us from danger or harm. Praise God that He alone has the power to save!

Praise

_____
_____
_____
_____
_____

Repent
Help us, O God of our salvation! Help us for the glory of your name.
Save us and forgive our sins for the honor of your name.
Psalm 79:9 (NLT)

God Saves

Acknowledge

_____
_____
_____
_____
_____
_____

Yield

_____
_____
_____
_____
_____
_____

The LORD is my rock, my fortress, and my savior;
my God is my rock, in whom I find protection. He is my shield,
the power that saves me, and my place of safety.
Psalm 18:2 (NLT)

How did God respond to this prayer?

_____
_____
_____
_____
_____
_____

God is Sovereign

Sovereign: supreme ruler; possessing supreme or ultimate power; free from external control

O Sovereign Lord! You made the heavens and earth by your strong hand and powerful arm. Nothing is too hard for you!
Jeremiah 32:17 (NLT)

Often when we describe something, we compare it to something similar. For example to describe the size of a giraffe, we might say, "It is almost as tall as a tree." When we try to describe the greatness of God, there is nothing we can compare Him to. God is above all things. He alone is unequalled in power and wisdom. There is nothing that He cannot do. Praise God that although He is the sovereign ruler of the universe, He loves you supremely!

Praise

_____

_____

_____

_____

_____

Repent

This is what the Sovereign Lord, the Holy One of Israel, says:
"In repentance and rest is your salvation."
Isaiah 30:15a (NIV)

God is Sovereign

Acknowledge

_____
_____
_____
_____
_____
_____

Yield

_____
_____
_____
_____
_____

But as for me, how good it is to be near God!
I have made the Sovereign LORD my shelter,
and I will tell everyone about the wonderful things you do.
Psalm 73:28 (NLT)

How did God respond to this prayer?

_____
_____
_____
_____
_____
_____

God sent a Substitute

Substitute: a person or thing serving or used in place of another

For God made Christ, who never sinned, to be the offering for our sin,
so that we could be made right with God through Christ.
2 Corinthians 5:21 (NLT)

In sports, when a critical game is played, often the substitute sits on the bench. The starters play until they are exhausted, then the coach sends in the substitutes to take their place. The game may be won or lost depending on the skill of the substitutes. In the Old Testament we read about all the rules and laws that God required for sin to be forgiven. God set up these rules to show that it is impossible to follow them perfectly. God knew we could not win against the power of sin, so He provided a way that the penalty for sin could be paid once for all. He sent a substitute to take our place. Jesus was the perfect Substitute, for He won the victory over sin. Praise God for Jesus, our Substitute.

Praise

_____
_____
_____
_____

Repent
But Christ has rescued us from the curse pronounced by the law. When
he was hung on the cross, he took upon himself the curse for our
wrongdoing. Galatians 3:13-14 (NLT)

God sent a Substitute

Acknowledge

_____
_____
_____
_____
_____
_____

Yield

_____
_____
_____
_____
_____

What we do see is Jesus, who was given a position "a little lower than the angels;" and because he suffered death for us, he is now "crowned with glory and honor." Yes, by God's grace, Jesus tasted death for everyone. Hebrews 2:9 (NLT)

How did God respond to this prayer?

_____
_____
_____
_____
_____
_____

Date: _____

God is Trustworthy

Trustworthy: dependable; reliable; worthy of placing confidence in or to put fully in charge

Those who know your name trust in you,
for you, O LORD, do not abandon those who search for you.
Psalm 9:10 (NLT)

Learning to put your trust in a friend requires that you spend time with them. You learn about their character by the way they speak and act. We learn about God's character by reading the Bible. Over and over again, God proves Himself to be trustworthy. As you have focused on many of God's attributes in this book, and as you see Him respond to your prayers, it becomes evident that God is always trustworthy. Praise God and put your trust in Him.

Praise

_____
_____
_____
_____
_____
_____
_____

Repent

This is a trustworthy saying, and everyone should accept it:
"Christ Jesus came into the world to save sinners."
1 Timothy 1:15a (NLT)

God is Trustworthy

Acknowledge

_____
_____
_____
_____
_____
_____

Yield

_____
_____
_____
_____
_____

Trust in the LORD with all your heart;
do not depend on your own understanding.
Seek his will in all you do, and he will show you which path to take.
Proverbs 3:5-6 (NLT)

How did God respond to this prayer?

_____
_____
_____
_____
_____
_____

God is Truth

Truth: that which is true; the quality of being consistent with experience, facts or reality; consistent with God's special revelation

And you will know the truth,
and the truth will set you free. John 8:32 (NLT)

The definition of truth seems to leave some room for interpretation. As our experiences differ, or as we interpret the facts of various situations, what is considered truth may vary. However, when we add this phrase to the definition "consistent with God's special revelation," the definition of truth becomes solid. Truth can clearly be established on the solid foundation of God's Word. So often, the enemy feeds our mind or fills our heart with half-truths that he designs to destroy our faith. Yet, if we use the truth of God's Word to defend ourselves against the half-truths or lies of the enemy, He sets us free and we are victorious. Praise God! He is truth.

Praise

_____
_____
_____
_____

Repent

If we claim we have no sin, we are only fooling ourselves
and not living in the truth. 1 John 1:8 (NLT)

God is Truth

Acknowledge

_____
_____
_____
_____
_____
_____

Yield

_____
_____
_____
_____
_____

Show me the right path, O LORD; point out the road for me to follow.
Lead me by your truth and teach me, for you are the God
who saves me. All day long I put my hope in you.
Psalm 25:4-6 (NLT)

How did God respond to this prayer?

_____
_____
_____
_____
_____
_____

God is Unchanging

Unchanging: remaining the same; consistent; not changing

Whatever is good and perfect is a gift coming down to us from God our
Father, who created all the lights in the heavens.
He never changes or casts a shifting shadow.
James 1:17 (NLT)

The sun and even the moon at times will cast a shadow of an object or a person. If that object moves even slightly, the shadow shifts and changes. This verse tells us that God is not like a shadow that changes; He is always the same. We can trust that He will always love us, always provide for our needs, always guide and protect us because He does not change. Praise God that He is unchanging!

Praise

_____
_____
_____
_____
_____

Repent

Let the wicked change their ways and banish the very thought of doing
wrong. Let them turn to the LORD that he may have mercy on them.
Yes, turn to our God, for he will forgive generously.
Isaiah 55:7 (NLT)

God is unchanging

Acknowledge

_____

_____

_____

_____

_____

_____

Yield

_____

_____

_____

_____

_____

Jesus Christ is the same yesterday, today, and forever.
Hebrews 13:8 (NLT)

How did God respond to this prayer?

_____

_____

_____

_____

_____

_____

_____

God understands

Understand: to comprehend; to know thoroughly; to have a sympathetic awareness

How great is our Lord! His power is absolute!
His understanding is beyond comprehension!
Psalm 147:5 (NLT)

Many times we ask God, "Why?" Our understanding of His work in our lives leaves us with questions. God explains in Isaiah 55:8-9 (NLT) *"My thoughts are nothing like your thoughts," says the LORD. "And my ways are far beyond anything you could imagine. For just as the heavens are higher than the earth, so my ways are higher than your ways and my thoughts higher than your thoughts."* With our limited knowledge and wisdom, we must trust God that He is working for our good. Rather than "Why?" our question should be, "What? What are you teaching me?" Praise God that He understands everything about you!

Praise

_____

_____

_____

_____

_____

Repent

And this is what he says to all humanity: "The fear of the Lord is true
wisdom; to forsake evil is real understanding."
Job 28:28 (NLT)

God Understands

Acknowledge

_____
_____
_____
_____
_____
_____

Yield

_____
_____
_____
_____
_____

Cry out for insight, and ask for understanding. Search for them
as you would for silver; seek them like hidden treasures.
Then you will understand what it means to fear the LORD,
and you will gain knowledge of God. For the LORD grants wisdom!
From his mouth come knowledge and understanding.
Proverbs 2:3-6 (NLT)

How did God respond to this prayer?

_____
_____
_____
_____

God is Victorious

Victorious: one who overcomes in a battle or struggle; having won a victory; triumphant

As your name deserves, O God, you will be praised to the ends of the earth. Your strong right hand is filled with victory.
Psalm 48:10 (NLT)

Have you ever been discouraged as you experienced a personal battle? We must realize that we will all face battles in life and that victory does not come without a battle. Jesus fought the battle against sin and death and He was victorious. Just as God was with Him, God is with us, giving us strength to stand firm and trust Him to fight the battle. Praise God, He is always victorious!

Praise

_____
_____
_____
_____
_____
_____
_____

Repent

But thank God! He gives us victory over sin and death through our Lord Jesus Christ.
1 Corinthians 15:57 (NLT)

God is Victorious

Acknowledge

_____
_____
_____
_____
_____
_____

Yield

_____
_____
_____
_____
_____

Don't be afraid, for I am with you. Don't be discouraged,
for I am your God. I will strengthen you and help you.
I will hold you up with my victorious right hand.
Isaiah 41:10 (NLT)

How did God respond to this prayer?

_____
_____
_____
_____
_____
_____

Date: _____

God is Wise

Wise: having wisdom; the power of good judgment; discerning; properly accessing what is true or right

Oh, how great are God's riches and wisdom and knowledge! How impossible it is for us to understand his decisions and his ways! For everything comes from him and exists by his power and is intended for his glory. All glory to him forever! Amen.
Romans 11:33,36 (NLT)

It truly is difficult to comprehend the infinite wisdom of God. Unlike the rulers of this world who have limited wisdom, God, who created the universe, has ALL wisdom. He is not limited by time and He sees all things from the perspective of eternity. We are blessed because we are His children. Praise God, for He is wise and we can put our faith and trust in Him at all times.

Praise

_____

_____

_____

_____

_____

Repent

Don't be impressed with your own wisdom.
Instead, fear the LORD and turn away from evil.
Proverbs 3:7 (NLT)

154

God is Wise

Acknowledge

_____

_____

_____

_____

_____

_____

Yield

_____

_____

_____

_____

_____

Fear of the LORD is the foundation of true wisdom. All who obey his commandments will grow in wisdom. Praise him forever!
Psalm 111:10 (NLT)

How did God respond to this prayer?

_____

_____

_____

_____

_____

_____

God is Worthy

Worthy: deserving respect, praise or attention; outstanding worth or importance

I will praise you every day; yes, I will praise you forever. Great is the LORD! He is most worthy of praise! No one can measure his greatness.
Let each generation tell its children of your mighty acts;
let them proclaim your power.
Psalm 145:2-4 (NLT)

As you focus on the attributes of God presented in this book, it is clear that He is excellent in His love, His wisdom, His knowledge, His faithfulness, His truth – there is no end to His excellence. He is above all. Nothing compares to Him. Praise God, for HE IS WORTHY!!

Praise

_____
_____
_____
_____

Repent

"I baptize with water those who repent of their sins and turn to God.
But someone is coming soon who is greater than I am—so much
greater that I'm not worthy even to be his slave and carry his sandals.
He will baptize you with the Holy Spirit and with fire."
Matthew 3:11 (NLT)

God is Worthy

Acknowledge

_____
_____
_____
_____
_____
_____

Yield

_____
_____
_____
_____
_____

For this reason, since the day we heard about you, we have not stopped praying for you. We continually ask God to fill you with the knowledge of his will through all the wisdom and understanding that the Spirit gives, so that you may live a life worthy of the Lord and please him in every way: bearing fruit in every good work, growing in the knowledge of God. Colossians 1:9-10 (NIV)

How did God respond to this prayer?

_____
_____
_____
_____
_____

Romans Road
The Plan of Salvation

If you have not received the free gift of salvation, your story can begin today.

Romans 10:17 (NIV) says:

Consequently, faith comes from hearing the message, and the message is heard through the word about Christ.

The following scriptures from the New Living Translation of God's Word, the Bible, show us God's plan of salvation.

Romans 3:23 *For everyone has sinned; we all fall short of God's glorious standard.*

Romans 6:23 *For the wages of sin is death, but the **free gift** of God is eternal life through Christ Jesus our Lord.*

Romans 5:8 *But God showed his great love for us by sending Christ to die for us while we were still sinners.*

Romans 10:9-10 *If you confess with your mouth that Jesus is Lord and believe in your heart that God raised him from the dead, you will be saved. For it is by believing in your heart that you are made right with God, and it is by confessing with your mouth that you are saved.*

Romans 10:13 *For "Everyone who calls on the name of the LORD will be saved."*

John 3:16 *For God loved the world so much that he gave his one and only Son, so that everyone who believes in him will not perish but have eternal life.*

God's Word explains that God loves you and wants to have a relationship with you. He loves you so much that He provides everything you need to establish that relationship. He provided His Son to pay the penalty for your sin. He has given you His Word to show the way of salvation. He gives the gift of faith that you might receive Jesus Christ as your Savior. He gives the Holy Spirit to be your constant guide.

If you believe God's word and would like to invite Jesus Christ into your life as your Savior, pray a simple prayer similar to this:

Dear God, I know I am a sinner. Please forgive me of my sins. I believe Jesus died and paid the penalty for my sins and rose again. I ask Jesus to come into my heart and I accept Him as Lord and Savior of my life. Thank you for saving me and giving me a relationship with you here on earth and eternal life with you in heaven. Amen

Before I received Jesus Christ as my Savior, I was unsure of eternal life with God in heaven. If you have believed, prayed and received God's gift of salvation, His Word gives us this assurance:

John 1:12 (NIV) *Yet to all who did receive him, to those who believed in his name, he gave the right to become children of God.*

1 John 5:13 (NLT) *I have written this to you who believe in the name of the Son of God, so that you may know you have eternal life.*

2 Corinthians 5:17(NLT) *This means that anyone who belongs to Christ has become a new person. The old life is gone; a new life has begun!*

Now you are a part of God's family. You can enjoy a relationship with God as his child. If you have received the gift of salvation, record today's date and on the following page write your story, then share it with someone. Continue praising God, repenting of sin, acknowledging His blessings and yielding your cares and concerns in prayer.

159

My Salvation Story

Today, _____, I invited Jesus Christ into my
heart to be my Savior and Lord. This is my story:

_____

_____

_____

_____

_____

_____

_____

_____

_____

_____

_____

And now, just as you accepted Christ Jesus as your Lord,
you must continue to follow him. Let your roots grow down into him,
and let your lives be built on him. Then your faith will grow strong
in the truth you were taught, and you will overflow with thankfulness.
Colossians 2:6-7(NLT)

Don't worry about anything; instead, pray about everything.
Tell God what you need, and thank him for all he has done.
Then you will experience God's peace,
which exceeds anything we can understand.
His peace will guard your hearts and minds as you live in Christ Jesus.
Philippians 4:6-7(NLT)

Books by Carol Graves

Four Steps to Peace – The Journey

This Bible study, focused on God's Word, has both refreshed and transformed the prayer life of many. An in-depth scriptural journey focusing on four steps of prayer: Praise – Repent – Acknowledge – Yield helps point the way to lasting peace.

Fully in Focus – A Scriptural Collection
Illustrating the Attributes of God

Fully in Focus – Discovering the Fullness of God

These devotional books each illustrate 52 attributes of God. The definitions, personal notes and Scripture references encourage a deeper knowledge of God's character. These helpful tools equip those who want to focus on the fullness of God as they experience the journey to peace. Carol has also authored five children's books, each designed to teach young children about God and His gift of salvation. Titles include:

Picture Books written in Rhyme

My First Glimpse of God
The Shining Star of Christmas
The Grumble Bug

Chapter Books for Early Readers

The Girl Who Wanted a Friend
The Boy Who Said, "I Can't!"

All books are available for order at
www.fullyinfocus.com